WONDERS OF CANADA

Head-Smashed-In Buffalo Jump

Anna Rebus

Weigl

CALGARY
www.weigl.com

Published by Weigl Educational Publishers Limited
6325 10th Street SE
Calgary, Alberta
T2H 2Z9

Website: www.weigl.com

We acknowledge the financial support of the Government of Canada through the Book Publishing
Industry Development Program (BPIDP) for our publishing activities.

Library and Archives Canada Cataloguing in Publication

Rebus, Anna
    Head-Smashed-In Buffalo Jump / Anna Rebus.

(Wonders of Canada)
Includes index.
ISBN 978-1-55388-389-0 (bound)
ISBN 978-1-55388-390-6 (pbk.)

    1. Head-Smashed-In Buffalo Jump Provincial Historic Site
(Alta.)--Juvenile literature. 2. Indians of North America--
Alberta--History--Juvenile literature. 3. World Heritage
areas--Alberta--Juvenile literature. I. Title. II. Series.
E78.A34R37 2007   j971.23'4   C2007-902258-8

Printed in the United States of America
1 2 3 4 5 6 7 8 9 0 11 10 09 08 07

Photograph Credits

Every reasonable effort has been made to trace ownership and to obtain permission to reprint copyright material. The publishers would be pleased to have any errors or omissions brought to their attention so that they may be corrected in subsequent printings.

Glenbow Archives: page 11 left (NA-2864-1228a); **QT Luong/terragalleria.com**: page 18.

All of the Internet URLs given in the book were valid at the time of publication. However, due to the dynamic nature of the Internet, some addresses may have changed, or sites may have ceased to exist since publication. While the author and publisher regret any inconvenience this may cause readers, no responsibility for any such changes can be accepted by either the author or the publisher.

Project Coordinator
Leia Tait

Design
Terry Paulhus

Contents

Plunge Into the Past 4

Where in the World? 6

A Trip Back in Time 8

Becoming a World Heritage Site 10

World Heritage in Canada 12

Natural Wonders 14

Cultural Treasures 16

Amazing Attractions 18

Issues in Heritage 20

Make a Story Robe 22

Quiz/Further Research 23

Glossary/Index 24

Plunge Into the Past

Imagine standing on an ancient cliff. Sandstone rocks crunch underfoot. Westerly winds scatter dust across the land. A few steps in front of you, the cliff drops away. A wide, flat prairie stretches many metres below. There, ancient tools and bone fragments are buried deep in the earth.

This is Head-Smashed-In **Buffalo Jump**, in southern Alberta. For thousands of years, it was used as a hunting site by **First Nations** Peoples. Today, Head-Smashed-In Buffalo Jump is one of the oldest and largest buffalo jumps in the world. Compared to other buffalo jumps, it is very well **preserved**. The site helps people understand how life in the area has changed over time. Head-Smashed-In Buffalo Jump was named a World Heritage Site in 1981.

■ Head-Smashed-In Buffalo Jump is a clear example of how First Nations Peoples used the land in creative ways to meet their needs.

What is a World Heritage Site?

Heritage is what people inherit from those who lived before them. It is also what they pass down to future generations. Heritage is made up of many things. Objects, traditions, beliefs, values, places, and people are all part of heritage. Throughout history, these things have been preserved. A family's heritage is preserved in the stories, customs, and objects its members pass on to each other. Similarly, a common human heritage is preserved in the beliefs, objects, and places that have special meaning for all people, such as Head-Smashed-In Buffalo Jump.

The United Nations Educational, Scientific and Cultural Organization (UNESCO) identifies places around the world that are important to all people. Some are important places in nature. Others are related to **culture**. These landmarks become World Heritage Sites. They are protected from being destroyed by **urbanization**, pollution, tourism, and neglect.

■ **Wildflowers, such as the prairie crocus, are part of the natural heritage found at Head-Smashed-In Buffalo Jump.**

You can learn more about UNESCO World Heritage Sites by visiting **http://whc.unesco.org**.

▶ Think about it ◀

World Heritage Sites belong to all people. They provide a link to the past. These sites also help people from many cultures connect with each other. Think about your own heritage. What landmarks are important to you? Think about the places that have shaped your life. Make a list of your personal heritage sites. The list might include your home, your grandparents' home, your school, or other place that is special to you and

Where in the World?

Head-Smashed-In Buffalo Jump is located in the Porcupine Hills region of southern Alberta. It is 18 kilometres northwest of the town of Fort MacLeod.

The buffalo jump site is large, covering 595 hectares of land. One of the largest parts of the site is the gathering basin. This is 40 square kilometres of grassland where herds of bison once grazed. Nearby, thousands of stone piles, called cairns, dot the landscape. These cairns form paths, called drive lanes, which lead toward a steep, sandstone cliff east of the gathering basin.

During a hunt, First Nations hunters chased bison down the drive lanes and over the cliff. Some of the animals were killed by the 10- to 18-metre fall to the plain below. Most were only stunned. First Nations hunters waited on the plain below the cliff to kill the animals. This area is now called the kill site. Below that was the processing site. Here, First Nations women prepared the bison to be made into food, clothing, and tools.

■ The landscape near Head-Smashed-In Buffalo Jump is made up of rolling hills and sandstone cliffs. Few trees grow in the area.

Puzzler

There are more than 100 buffalo jumps in North America. Most of Canada's jumps are located in the Interior Plains. This is one of seven **geographic** regions in Canada. Each region has special natural features, such as landforms, climate, plants, and wildlife. Use an atlas from your classroom or school library to learn more about Canada's geographic regions. Then, look at the list of regions below. Match the regions to the letters on the map.

ANSWERS: 1. C 2. F 3. B 4. G 5. E 6. A 7. D

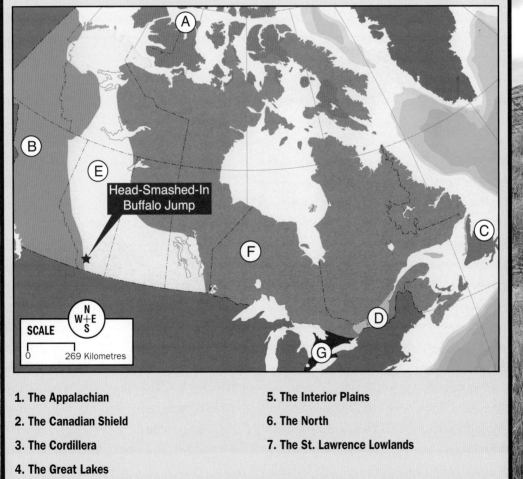

1. The Appalachian

2. The Canadian Shield

3. The Cordillera

4. The Great Lakes

5. The Interior Plains

6. The North

7. The St. Lawrence Lowlands

A Trip Back in Time

First Nations Peoples of the Plains believe that they have always lived on this land. Ancient tools and other evidence found by **archaeologists** show they have been there for at least 11,000 years. Many Plains groups, such as the Blackfoot, once depended on bison for their survival. Bison meat was their main source of food. They made clothing, shelter, tools, and weapons from the animals' hides, bones, horns, and hooves.

The Blackfoot had many ways of hunting bison. Using buffalo jumps was one of the most successful. Ancient bones found by archaeologists show that Head-Smashed-In was used as a buffalo jump at least 5,700 years ago. It was last used as a buffalo jump in the 1800s.

▬ Hunters watched the hunts from the top of the cliff. Once, a curious Blackfoot boy was crushed by falling bison while watching a hunt from the cliff base. Head-Smashed-In Buffalo Jump was named for him.

Site Science

To learn more about important heritage sites, archaeologists dig in the ground to uncover **artifacts**. First, they plot a grid pattern on the ground. Then, they scrape away thin layers of dirt in small, square sections. They take photographs and make detailed notes about the site and objects they find as they dig.

In 1938, Junius Bird of the American Museum of Natural History was the first archaeologist to **excavate** Head-Smashed-In Buffalo Jump. Since then, archaeologists have found thousands of bison bone fragments deep in the ground. In some areas, they have unearthed stone tools and other items made by First Nations Peoples. These findings have helped experts better understand how the site was used and how it changed over time.

▬ Four major digs took place at the jump between the 1940s and the 1990s.

FIND MORE ONLINE

Learn more about archaeologists and the work they do at
www.cr.nps.gov/archeology/public/kids.

Becoming a World Heritage Site

Between the 1940s and 1990s, four major archaeology digs took place at Head-Smashed-In Buffalo Jump. These studies brought a great deal of attention to the site. They helped people better understand its historical importance. As a result, the Government of Canada made Head-Smashed-In Buffalo Jump a National Historic Site in 1968. National Historic Sites recognize people, places, and events that are important in Canadian history. Laws protect these sites from being torn down or changed in any major way.

In the 1970s, the Canadian Government brought Head-Smashed-In Buffalo Jump to UNESCO's attention. Government experts noted that Head-Smashed-In is the best-preserved buffalo jump in the world. They used archaeological findings to show that the site is important to Aboriginal history around the world. UNESCO agreed. The group made Head-Smashed-In Buffalo Jump a World Heritage Site on October 30, 1981.

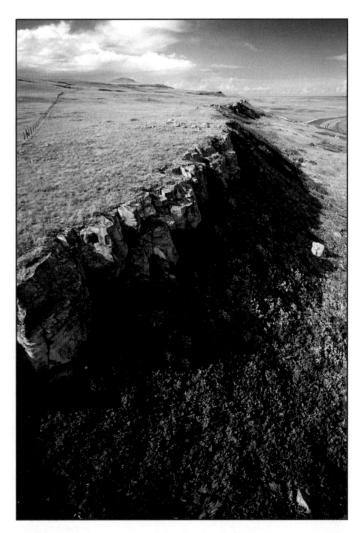

■ **Head-Smashed-In Buffalo Jump contains more archaeological history than any other buffalo jump in the world.**

Heritage Heroes

Dr. Richard Forbis was a well-known Alberta archaeologist. In 1957, he joined the the Glenbow Foundation, now the Glenbow Museum, in Calgary. There, Dr. Forbis took part in many Alberta archaeology projects.

During the 1960s, Dr. Forbis and Dr. Brian Reeves excavated Head-Smashed-In Buffalo Jump. Their findings helped determine the age of the site. They also showed that the site was used more during some periods of history than others.

Dr. Forbis researched and wrote many articles about Head-Smashed-In Buffalo Jump. He urged the Alberta government to protect the site and helped develop the Alberta Historical Resources Act. The act outlines how important historical sites in Alberta should be identified, preserved, and protected by law. Along with Head-Smashed-In Buffalo Jump, Dr. Forbis helped to preserve many important archaeological sites in Alberta. He is often called the "Father of Alberta Archaeology."

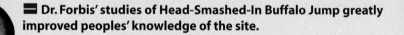

Dr. Forbis' studies of Head-Smashed-In Buffalo Jump greatly improved peoples' knowledge of the site.

World Heritage in

CANADA

There are more than 800 UNESCO World Heritage Sites in 138 countries around the globe. Canada has 14 of these sites. Seven are natural sites, and seven are cultural sites. Each is believed to be of outstanding heritage value to all people around the world. Look at the map. Are any of these sites near your home? Have you visited any of them? Learn more about World Heritage Sites in Canada by visiting www.pc.gc.ca/progs/spm-whs/itm2-/index_e.asp.

UNITED STATES
OF AMERICA

YUKON

⑥

⑨

BRITISH
COLUMBIA

⑫

ALBERTA

①

④ ②

⑬

LEGEND

◯ = Natural Landmarks

● = Cultural Sites

N
W+E
S

SCALE

0   269 Kilometres

L'Anse aux Meadows National Historic Site (Newfoundland and Labrador)
- The site of the first European settlement in North America, founded in 1,000 AD
- The first World Heritage Site declared in Canada

Miguasha National Park (Quebec)
- The world's most important deposit of marine fossils
- Features 370 million-year-old remains of the fish that were the ancestors of the first animals to breathe air

Nahanni National Park Reserve (Northwest Territories)
- Home to the South Nahanni River, which travels through unique landforms, such as deep canyons, towering waterfalls, and a complex limestone cave system

① Canadian Rocky Mountain Parks (Alberta and British Columbia)

② Dinosaur Provincial Park (Alberta)

③ Gros Morne National Park (Newfoundland and Labrador)

④ Head-Smashed-In Buffalo Jump (Alberta)

CANADA

NORTHWEST
TERRITORIES

NUNAVUT

(14)

SASKATCHEWAN

MANITOBA

NEWFOUNDLAND
AND LABRADOR

(7)

(3)

ONTARIO

QUEBEC

PRINCE
EDWARD
ISLAND

(8)

NEW
BRUNSWICK

NOVA
SCOTIA

UNITED STATES
OF AMERICA

(5)

(10)

(11)

5 The Historic District of
Old-Quebec (Quebec)

6 Kluane/Wrangell-St Elias/Glacier
Bay/Tatshenshini-Alsek (British
Columbia, Yukon, and Alaska)

7 L'Anse aux Meadows National
Historic Site (Newfoundland

8 Miguasha National Park (Quebec)

9 Nahanni National Park Reserve
(Northwest Territories)

10 Old Town Lunenburg (Nova Scotia)

11 Rideau Canal (Ontario)

12 SGang Gwaay (British Columbia)

13 Waterton Glacier International
Peace Park (Alberta and Montana)

14 Wood Buffalo National Park
(Alberta and Northwest Territories)

Natural Wonders

Head-Smashed-In Buffalo Jump sits on the southeastern edge of the Porcupine Hills. This is a hilly region in southern Alberta that lies between the Prairies and the Rocky Mountains. The Porcupine Hills are the only place in the province where four distinct vegetation types grow together in one region. These are montane forest, subalpine forest, aspen parkland, and prairie grassland. The area around Head-Smashed-In Buffalo Jump is made up of mostly grassland plants.

Head-Smashed-In Buffalo Jump overlooks the Oldman River valley. The Oldman River flows out of the Rocky Mountains in southwest Alberta. As it flows from the mountains to the prairies, it joins with the Bow River to form the South Saskatchewan River. The Oldman River is 362 kilometres long. It supplies water to the city of Lethbridge and the town of Fort MacLeod.

The Porcupine Hills are named for Douglas fir and limber pine trees that grow on the hilltops. The pointy treetops look like quills poking up from a porcupine's back.

FIND MORE ONLINE

Learn more about the Oldman River by visiting **www.alberta source.ca/alphabet**. Click on the "o" in the alphabet. Then, click on "Oldman River."

Creature Feature

Bison are the largest land animals in North America. They stand about 2 metres tall and weigh nearly 1,000 kilograms. Bison have brown shaggy coats, short horns, and a large hump on their shoulders. They are herd animals, so they live in large groups.

Bison are often called buffalo. This was the term early European explorers used to describe these animals. Jump sites in North America are still known as buffalo jumps, not bison jumps, because the term is so common.

Bison are important animals in Canadian history. Before Europeans came to the Plains, First Nations Peoples depended on bison for their survival. At that time, as many as 70 million bison roamed the land. By the late 1870s, bison were almost **extinct** due to over-hunting. During the 1900s, some people raised bison on special farms to help increase their numbers. Today, about 90,000 bison live in Canada and the United States.

▬ **Today, large herds of bison roam on lands protected by the Canadian government.**

Cultural Treasures

Blackfoot Peoples continue to live in the area around Head-Smashed-In Buffalo Jump. The Blackfoot have many names for themselves including *Niitsitapi*, which means "The Real People," and *Sao-kitapiiksi*, which means "The Plains People."

The Blackfoot are made up of three different **clans**. They are the Siksika (Blackfoot), the Kainai (also called the Blood), and the Piikani (Peigan). Together, these clans make up the Blackfoot **Confederacy**.

Today, Blackfoot culture thrives at Head-Smashed-In Buffalo Jump. Many people who work at the site have Blackfoot heritage. They often perform traditional songs, dances, and drum music. They demonstrate Blackfoot arts, crafts, and tool making, and share traditional stories. They also teach others about Blackfoot traditions through movies, music recordings, digital photography, and the Internet.

■ In the past, the Blackfoot made "story robes" by painting pictures onto bison hides. A robe could tell the history of one person, or it could tell one person's version of a clan's history.

Telling Tales

The Blackfoot use storytelling to teach children and others about their history and culture. Buffalo Calling Stones is a story about the Blackfoot connection to the bison.

One season, the Blackfoot were very hungry. The herds of bison had disappeared. Everyone was starving. One day, a lady named Weasel Woman was collecting water from a river near her camp. She heard something calling to her from the bushes. When she looked closer, Weasel Woman found a stone. The stone spoke to her. It said, "Take me. Take me. I have great power." The stone taught Weasel Woman a song she could sing to call the bison.

Weasel Woman took the stone back to camp. She taught the elders the song to call the bison. The elders sang the song. The calling stone sang with them. Before long, everyone heard the thunder of bison hoofs on the plain. The hunters ran beside the bison. They drove the herd over a nearby cliff. Everyone had plenty of meat and many hides for new lodge covers. Since then, the Blackfoot have found other calling stones. They keep the stones safe and call on them when they need help.

Amazing Attractions

A visit to Head-Smashed-In Buffalo Jump usually begins with a walk through the **Interpretive Centre**. Here, educational displays and activities teach visitors about the buffalo jump, archaeological discoveries, bison, and Blackfoot culture. At certain times of the year, visitors can try making hand drums, stone tools, or Blackfoot foods such as **pemmican.** A theatre also shows movies about First Nations Peoples.

Outdoors, many paths allow visitors to explore certain areas of the jump site on their own. Guided hikes are available through the drive lanes and the gathering basin. During the warm summer months, visitors can camp in teepees below the sandstone cliffs at the site. Campers can hear traditional Blackfoot stories told around the campfire.

▰ First Nations guides at Head-Smashed-In Buffalo Jump provide visitors with information about specific areas of the site and their uses.

Featured Attraction

The Interpretive Centre at Head-Smashed-In Buffalo Jump opened in 1987. It is a work of art. The centre was built directly into the side of the cliff to blend in with the natural landscape of the site. Its location was carefully chosen so that the building would not disturb any artifacts at the site.

To build the centre, large amounts of dirt were removed from the cliff. When the building was complete, dirt and grass were laid over it.

Issues in Heritage

In the past, Head-Smashed-In Buffalo Jump was not protected. As a result, people caused damage to parts of the site. When settlers first came to the area in the late 1800s, some areas of the gathering basin were used as farmland. Ponds for watering livestock were built below the cliffs. In the late 1880s, a wagon road was built at the cliff face. Settlers also removed sandstone from the cliff for building material.

Today, Head-Smashed-In Buffalo Jump is well protected, but it may face some challenges in the future. For example, the site may have fewer visitors. This is a problem at heritage sites across Canada. Many people spend their free time watching movies and playing video games instead of visiting these sites. To attract more visitors to Head-Smashed-In Buffalo Jump, some people want to keep bison at the site. Bison are not kept at the site right now because it would be costly and difficult for site staff to care for the animals. However, more people might visit the site if they could see bison roaming the land as they did for thousands of years in the past.

■ Today, most of the grassland near Head-Smashed-In Buffalo Jump is used for grazing animals from nearby farms.

FIND MORE ONLINE

You can help protect Head-Smashed-In Buffalo Jump and other World Heritage Sites at: http://whc.unesco.org/education.

Should Head-Smashed-In Buffalo Jump bring bison to the site to attract more visitors?

YES	NO
 Bison once roamed free in this area. They are part of the prairie environment, and they should be at the site.	Keeping bison at the site would cost a great deal of money and require more staff to take care of the animals.
More tourists might come to Head-Smashed-In Buffalo Jump to see bison up close.	 In Alberta, there are other places where people can see bison in their natural habitat, such as Elk Island National Park.
 Having bison at the site would give visitors an excellent opportunity to learn more about bison from local First Nations Peoples.	No further development should occur at Head-Smashed-In Buffalo Jump. The site should be left alone because it is a protected heritage site.

Think about this issue. Are there any possible solutions that would satisfy both sides of the debate?

Make a Story Robe

Story robes were an important way for Blackfoot Peoples to record their history. Often, individuals made story robes to record important events in their own lives. Make your own story robe by using pictures to tell about the main events in your life.

Materials Needed
One large sheet of sturdy light brown or beige paper (at least 30 centimetres by 40 centimetres), scissors, and crayons, coloured markers, or pastels

 Use scissors to cut around the edges of the paper so it looks like the shape of a bison hide.

 Choose at least five important events in your life that you want to show on your story robe.

 Plan how you will draw your life stories on the paper. You can draw your pictures in rows, in groups, or at random on the page.

 Use crayons, coloured markers, or pastels to draw pictures representing important events in your life.

 Once your story robe is finished, write down what your symbols mean. Share your story robe with your class.

Quiz

1. When was Head-Smashed-In Buffalo Jump made a World Heritage Site?
2. True or false? The Denesuline First Nations group is connected to Head-Smashed-In Buffalo Jump.
3. True or false? Head-Smashed-In Buffalo Jump was last used in the 1400s.
4. Where is Head-Smashed-In Buffalo Jump located?
5. True or false? Bison live in groups.

ANSWERS: 1. October 30, 1981   2. False. The Blackfoot are connected to Head-Smashed-In Buffalo Jump.   3. False. Head-Smashed-In Buffalo Jump was last used in the mid-1800s.   4. Alberta   5. true

Further Research

You can find more information about Head-Smashed-In Buffalo Jump at your local library or on the Internet.

Libraries

Most libraries have computers that connect to a database for researching information. If you input a key word, you will be provided with a list of books in the library that contain information on that topic. Non-fiction books are arranged numerically, using their call number. Fiction books are organized alphabetically by the author's last name.

Websites

Take a virtual tour of Head-Smashed-In Buffalo Jump at **www.head-smashed-in.com**.

Discover the Blackfoot way of life by visiting **www.glenbow.org/blackfoot**.

Glossary

archaeologists: scientists who study objects from the past to learn about the people who made and used them

artifacts: objects used or made by humans long ago

buffalo jump: a place where Plains First Nations groups hunted bison by chasing them over a cliff

clans: groups of people that share common ancestors

confederacy: a league of persons, parties, or states

culture: the arts, beliefs, habits, and institutions of a specific community, people, or nation

excavate: to carefully dig up buried objects to find information about the past

extinct: a species of animal that no longer exists

First Nations: members of Canada's Aboriginal community who are not Inuit or Métis

geographic: related to the study of Earth's surface and its natural features

interpretive centre: a place where visitors learn about certain topics through educational displays

pemmican: a mixture of dried meat and berries mixed with fat

preserved: protected from injury, loss, or ruin

urbanization: the movement of people out of the countryside and into cities

Index

archaeologists 8, 9, 11
archaeology 10, 11, 18
artifacts 9, 19
attractions 18, 19

Bird, Junius 9
bison 6, 8, 9, 15, 16, 17, 18, 20, 21, 22, 23
Blackfoot 8, 16, 17, 18, 22, 23

culture 5, 16, 17, 18

First Nations 4, 6, 8, 9, 15, 18, 21, 23
Forbis, Richard George 11

history 5, 8, 9, 10, 11, 15, 16, 17, 20

Interior Plains 7
Interpretive Centre 18, 19
issues 20, 21

Oldman River 14

pemmican 18
Porcupine Hills 6, 14

story robes 16, 22
storytelling 17, 18

United Nations Educational, Scientific and Cultural Organization (UNESCO) 5, 10, 12, 20

World Heritage Sites 4, 5, 10, 12, 13, 20, 23